Honey Bees at Work

Marilyn Woolley

Momentum
Honey-bees at Work

First published in Great Britain in 1999 by

Folens Publishers
Albert House
Apex Business Centre
Boscombe Road
Dunstable
Beds LU5 4RL

British Library Cataloguing in Publication Data.
A Catalogue record for this book is available from the British Library

ISBN 1 86202 767 6

Designed by Pauline McClenahan
Printed in Singapore by PH Productions Pte Ltd

The author wishes to thank Graham Angus for information contributing to this book. Graham is a beekeeper from Sticky Fingers Honey Shop, Aireys Inlet.

Every effort has been made to contact the owners of the photographs in this book. Where this has not been possible, we invite the owners of the copyright to notify the publishers.

ANT Photo Library/Alan Gibb p. 6; ANT Photo Library/I.R. McCann Photo pp. 5, 29; ANT Photo Library/N.H.P.A. pp. 1, 4, 6(insert), 8(insert), 9, 12, 14, 17, 18, 19; ANT Photo Library/Otto Rogge cover, pp. 7, 8, 10, 15, 16(insert), 22, 24, 25, 26, 30; ANT Photo Library/Silvestris p. 11; ANT Photo Library/Dave Watts p. 27; ANT Photo Library/Cyril Webster pp. 13, 16; Keith Pigdon p. 28; Ken Stepnell p. 20.

Contents

Introduction

In spring and summer, honey-bees buzz through parks, orchards and fields. They look for a good source of nectar and pollen. Most of the day is spent making many trips from blossom to blossom. Then they hurry back to the hive with the food.

Back in the hive, the busy worker bee lives and works with up to 50 000 honey-bees. They live in a large family group, or colony. In each colony, there is one queen bee. There are also a few hundred male bees called drones, and thousands of female worker bees.

As she grows older, the female worker bee's duties in the hive change. She must work at all the different jobs in the hive until she is old enough for the important job of collecting honey and pollen. The first part of her life centres on the queen and her young.

Looking After the Queen and the Hive

The queen bee is larger than all the other bees in the hive. She has a large abdomen and spends almost all of her time in the hive laying eggs. In spring and summer, she lays more than one egg per minute as she crawls over the cells in the hive. Each egg is laid in a six-sided cell. Hundreds of these cells are joined together to make a honeycomb. The queen can lay up to 2000 eggs a day, and up to two million eggs in her lifetime of about five years.

Cleaning out empty cells

It is the job of the youngest worker bees to feed the queen and look after her as she lays the eggs. They also make sure that the temperature in the cells is right. They fan the cells with their wings to lower the temperature. Sometimes they huddle together to make it warmer. The young honey-bees clean the cells and carry waste out of the hive. They clean out old cells so they can be used again. They line each cell with a substance that kills germs.

At three days old, young honey-bees start feeding the larvae in the nursery. The blind, legless grubs spend most of their time eating. First, the nursery workers feed the grubs royal jelly. This is a rich, white substance produced by glands in the heads of the workers. The nursery workers then feed each grub a mixture of honey and pollen. This is called beebread. The grubs grow very quickly. When the grubs have finished feeding, older workers produce wax to make a cap over the top of each cell. This cap covers up the grub inside.

Within the cell, the grub spins a cocoon of silk. This becomes a pupa. Soon after, the grub changes into its adult form. It chews its way through the wax cap. Once out, the bee spreads its antennae and wings.

After they have had their turn in the nursery, young bees become builders. By the time they are ten days old, they are able to produce wax. They can start helping to construct and repair the cells that make up the hive.

Making new cells

The wax they use comes out in tiny flakes from the underside of their abdomens. They mould these into the shape required. They use these either for a cap to seal a grub into a cell or for making new cells. The bees join these new cells together to make the honeycomb larger. The queen will lay more eggs in the cells, or they will be used for storing honey.

After a few days as builders, the worker bees finally venture out of the hive. They use their first flight to become familiar with the hive's surroundings.

When they are about three weeks old, honey-bees have their turn at guard duty. The hive needs to be guarded so that only bees belonging to the hive can come in.

The guards recognise other members of the colony by smell. Each hive has its own special odour. A bee that does not belong to the hive will be chased away by the guards. It will be stung if necessary.

Finally, the honey-bees become collectors. This is the job they will do for the rest of their lives.

At the hive's entrance, every incoming bee is checked by the guards.

The Work of the Collector Bee

In spring and summer, as the morning sun comes up, collector bees leave their hives. They fly out to the flowers and trees in blossom. The buzzing noise they make as they fly is caused by the rapid beating of their two pairs of wings.

When a collector bee reaches a blossoming tree, she flies from flower to flower. She uses her antennae to feel and smell. She uses a long, thin mouthpiece called a proboscis to sip the nectar from the flowers. The nectar goes into a special chamber near the bee's stomach. This is called a honey stomach. There, it mixes with juices and becomes a watery honey mixture.

As she moves over the flowers, pollen sticks to the tiny hairs all over her body, legs and antennae. She uses her front and middle legs to brush off this pollen. She moves it into two areas called pollen baskets on her hind legs. The pollen baskets are smooth areas covered with long hairs. After she has visited hundreds of flowers, these two baskets become full. It is then time for her to fly back to the hive with her honey and pollen.

When she returns to the hive, the collector bee moves the pollen out of her pollen baskets. She puts it into some of the wax cells. She then brings up the honey mixture and passes it on to the younger hive workers. These bees put the honey mixture into other wax cells in the honeycomb.

As the honey is put into the cells, the younger hive workers fan their wings over it so that some of the water dries up. When each honey cell is full, it is sealed with a thin cap of wax.

The honey and pollen are eaten by the bees in the hive. Honey gives bees energy. Pollen gives them protein, fats, vitamins and minerals.

Comb cells filled with pollen

Every day, each busy collector bee flies up to five kilometres to gather food. She is able to do this because of her light body. Her diet of honey and pollen provides her with lots of energy. On these long flights, she will rest for about 15 minutes every two hours. She will make thousands of trips to gather enough nectar to make less than five grams of honey. When she finds a good source of nectar, she will let the other bees know where it is.

The Dance of the Honeybee

When a collector bee finds flowers that contain nectar, she returns to the hive fully loaded with the food. There, she does a special dance on the surface of the honeycomb. This tells the other bees where the flowers are.

The other bees can tell what kind of plants they will be looking for by the smell that the collector bee brings into the hive. If the nectar is especially good, or if there is a large amount of it, the dancing collector bee does a longer, more lively dance and makes different sounds.

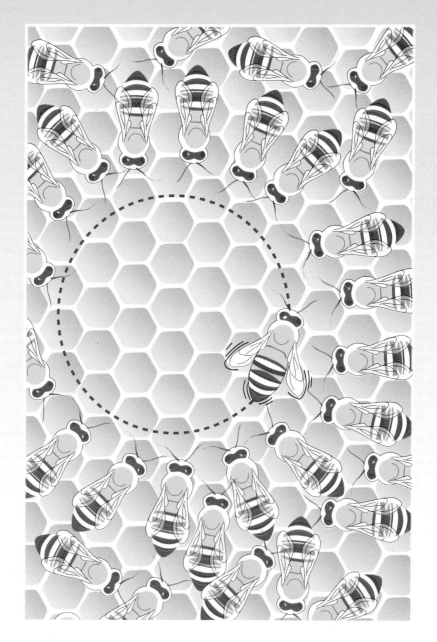

If the bee dances in a big circle, this tells the other collector bees that the flowers are close by, less than 90 metres away.

A tail-wagging dance in a figure-8 pattern tells the other collectors that the honey is farther away.

The tail-wagging dance also shows them the direction in which they must fly to find the flowers. If the bee dances upwards on the comb, the flowers are located toward the sun. If the bee dances downwards on the comb, the flowers are located away from the sun.

Tail-wagging dances are also performed when the hive becomes full of honey and some of the bees swarm out to start a new colony.

Swarming to a New Home

During a good season, the cells in the honeycomb become full of honey. The queen begins to lay more eggs. There is plenty of food for the grubs. When the young bees emerge, the colony becomes crowded with new worker bees. If there is no room to expand, some of the bees will have to leave to form a new colony. If there is to be a new colony, there needs to be a new queen.

A crowded hive

The queen *(centre)* passes queen substance to the workers as they tend her.

Throughout her life, the queen bee produces a smell that stops the worker bees from making new queens. This queen substance is spread throughout the hive by the workers near the queen as they pass food to the other workers. Every bee gets a little bit of queen substance passed on to them. This way, all the bees know that there is a queen present. When the hive is overcrowded, there is not enough queen substance to go around. Each bee gets less of the queen substance. The bees then sense that the queen is missing or ill.

When this happens, the nursery workers start to feed a few female grubs with only the rich royal jelly. This makes them grow faster, and they become queens. The workers turn the cells into queen cells by making them longer and wider. This means that the queen grubs have room to grow. Just before the new queens develop, the old queen takes some of the workers and flies off to start a new hive.

Between 5000 and 25 000 bees swarm out of the hive. The queen lands not far from the old hive. The workers all settle around her in a cluster. A few of the bees fly off to scout for a new site. When they find a suitable place, they return to the cluster. They perform the tail-wagging dance to let the others know where the new location is. The swarm takes off again to set up a new hive. The hive can be made in a hole in a tree-trunk or under a rock ledge.

Drones look just like
workers, but they
are bigger and fatter.

   Back in the old
hive, the new queens
are ready to emerge.
The first-born queen kills
the other queens before they come
out of their cells. If two or more queens are born
at the same time, they fight to the death. The
winner becomes the new queen of the colony.

   When she is about a week old, the new queen
flies out of the hive on her mating flight. She will
mate with one or more of the male bees, or
drones, from another colony. Drones are only
reared in summer when there is plenty of food.
They spend most of their time in the hive eating,
so they grow very fat. After about 12 days of
endless eating, they leave the hive. Their only job
is to find a queen and mate with her. Drones die
soon after they have mated.

As summer draws to a close and the blossoms grow into fruit, the activity in the hive dies down. Collector bees stop flying out to gather pollen and nectar. They cluster within the hive. The queen stops laying eggs. The honeycomb is full of enough honey to last through the winter.

Young bees that emerge now join the cluster of bees. They keep the hive warm by huddling together over the cells. They live on the honey they stored in the spring and summer.

When the weather begins to warm, the queen starts laying eggs again. Collector bees fly out to gather more food. Grubs start emerging, and the cycle repeats, with busy worker bees taking on their important duties throughout the hive.

Glossary

abdomen	one of the three sections of an insect's body
antennae	the pair of feelers on an insect's head
cell	a small compartment
cluster	a group of similar things in a bunch
construct	to build
hind legs	back legs
larvae	the young that hatch from insects' eggs
minerals	nutrients that come from the ground
nectar	the sweet liquid produced by many flowers
odour	a smell
orchards	fields of fruit trees
pollen	the fine dust on the centre of flowers
protein	a substance needed for all animal and plant life processes
pupa	the third stage of an insect's development, when it is in its cocoon
swarm	a great number of bees moving together
vitamins	essential nutrients

Index